The Real Deal

Alcohol

Rachel Lynette

Heinemann
LIBRARY

www.heinemann.co.uk/library
Visit our website to find out more information about **Heinemann** Library books.

To order:

 Phone 44 (0) 1865 888112

 Send a fax to 44 (0) 1865 314091

 Visit the Heinemann bookshop at www.heinemann.co.uk/library to browse our catalogue and order online.

First published in Great Britain by Heinemann Library, Halley Court, Jordan Hill, Oxford OX2 8EJ, part of Pearson Education.

Heinemann is a registered trademark of Pearson Education Ltd.

Editorial: Nancy Dickmann
Design: Richard Parker and Tinstar Design Ltd
Illustrations: Darren Lingard
Picture Research: Mica Brancic and Frances Topp
Production: Alison Parsons

Originated by Chroma Graphics
Printed and bound in China by Leo Paper Group

ISBN 978 0 431 90728 4 (hardback)
12 11 10 09 08

10 9 8 7 6 5 4 3 2 1

ISBN 978 0 431 90735 2 (paperback)
13 12 11 10 09

10 9 8 7 6 5 4 3 2 1

British Library Cataloguing in Publication Data
Lynette, Rachel
    Alcohol. - (The real deal)
    1. Alcohol - Physiological effect - Juvenile literature
    2. Alcohol - Juvenile literature
    I. Title
    613.8'1

A full catalogue record for this book is available from the British Library.

Acknowledgments
The publishers would like to thank the following for permission to reproduce photographs:
Bubbles/John Powell p. **19**; Corbis pp. **4** (Comstock), **9** (Richard Klune), **18** (Mike Watson); Getty Images pp. **7** (Hulton Archive/Stringer), **24** (Dorling Kindersley); Jupiter/Sharon L. Jonz p. **26**; Masterfile pp. **14** (Randal Ford), **20** (Siephoto), **22**, **25** (WireimageStock); PhotoLibrary/Banana Stock p. **27**; Photolibrary.com pp. **12** (Dynamic Graphics (UK) Ltd), **13** (Plainpicture Jackel O), **23** (Banana Stock); Science Photo Library pp. **16** right (CNRI), **16** left (SIU); SuperStock pp. **6**, **11** (Kwame Zikomo), **15**, **17** (Prisma), **21** (Vincent Hobbs/SPL); Ronald Grant Archive/Walt Disney Pictures/Jerry Bruckheimer Films p. **8**.

Cover photograph of an arrow road sign reproduced with permission of iStockphoto/Nicholas Belton.

The publishers would like to thank Kostadinka Grossmith for her assistance in the preparation of this book.

Every effort has been made to contact copyright holders of any material reproduced in this book. Any omissions will be rectified in subsequent printings if notice is given to the publishers.

Contents

Some words are shown in bold, **like this**. You can find out what they mean by looking in the glossary.

What is alcohol?

Alcohol is a chemical that is formed when plants **ferment.** Many drinks contain alcohol. Alcohol is a **depressant**. This means that it makes people feel relaxed and makes their bodies work slower. People drink alcohol to have these feelings.

Alcohol is poisonous in large amounts. If a person drinks a great deal of alcohol in a short period of time, he or she can die from alcohol poisoning. People rarely drink enough alcohol to cause death. However, alcohol can damage their body over time.

Some people become **addicted** to alcohol. They cannot control how much alcohol they drink. If they try to stop drinking alcohol, they experience strong **cravings** to drink.

NEWSFLASH

"Alcopops" are a relatively new kind of alcoholic drink that has become popular with young people. These drinks are alcoholic, but they resemble drinks such as lemonade and soft drinks. Alcopops have the same alcohol content as beer.

Alcohol comes in several different forms.

Each of the measures below contains one unit of alcohol.

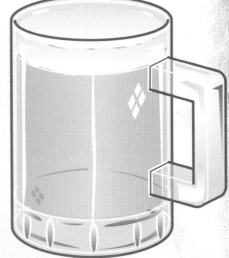

25 ml hard liquor = 125 ml wine = ½ pint (284 ml) beer

Alcoholic drinks

Most alcoholic drinks fall into one of three main categories. The different kinds of alcoholic drinks contain different amounts of alcohol.

Beer is made by fermenting grain, most commonly barley. Beer contains three to five percent alcohol. Although beer contains less alcohol than other kinds of alcoholic drinks, people usually drink more of it. A standard measure of beer is 1 pint (568 millilitres).

Wine is made by fermenting fruit, usually grapes. Wine contains nine to sixteen percent alcohol. Because wine has more alcohol than beer, people usually drink less wine. A standard glass of wine contains 125 millilitres.

Distilled spirits (sometimes called hard liquor) are made from grains and other plants. Whisky, rum, and vodka are distilled spirits. Distilled spirits contain much more alcohol than beer and wine – up to 50 percent. A standard drink of distilled spirits is just 25 millilitres.

Alcohol in society

Alcohol is part of most **cultures** around the world. About 75 percent of men and 60 percent of women in the United Kingdom drink alcohol at least once a week.

People might have an alcoholic drink with a meal. They might drink alcohol at weddings, parties, and other celebrations. In addition to making people feel relaxed, alcohol helps to put people at ease. It may make them feel friendlier, more talkative, and less self-conscious. This is why alcohol is so popular at social gatherings.

Alcohol is also a part of some religious ceremonies. Catholics use wine for their celebration of communion. Wine is also an important part of the Jewish holiday of Passover. However, some religions, such as Mormonism and Islam, do not permit their members to drink alcohol.

People often drink alcohol at parties or celebrations.

Alcohol and the law

Laws about alcohol vary from place to place. It is illegal for anyone under the age of 18 to buy alcoholic beverages in England. A 16- or 17-year-old can drink beer, wine, or cider with a meal if it is bought for them by someone over 18. In Scotland, 16- and 17-year-olds can buy beer, wine, or cider with a meal. The legal age for buying alcohol in Australia is also 18 years. It is illegal for any person under 18 to drink alcohol in a place that sells alcohol.

People who sell or give alcohol to people under the legal age limit can be subject to steep fines or even a prison sentence. Despite these laws, a survey in 2005 showed that 58 percent of 11–15 year olds had tried alcohol.

In the United States, selling alcohol was banned from 1920 to 1933. Illegal alcohol was destroyed.

What do you think?

Until November 2005, all bars in the United Kingdom had to close at the same set time. After this date, any bar with a special licence could serve alcohol 24 hours a day, every day. It was hoped that this would stop the chaos on the streets that was happening when all of the bars closed together. Do you think this was a good idea?

Alcohol in the media

People are often shown drinking alcohol on television and in films. The actors in these shows usually look like they are having fun. They make drinking alcohol look appealing. Studies have shown that celebrities have a big influence on teenagers. When teenagers see film and television stars drinking, it may make them want to drink too.

Popular films such as *Pirates of the Caribbean* can make being drunk seem funny.

What do you think?

Tobacco companies are not allowed to advertise their products on television. Many people think that alcohol companies should also be banned from television. Other people think the adverts are entertaining and that alcohol companies have as much right to advertise on television as anyone else. Do you think adverts for alcohol should be banned?

Alcohol adverts

Alcohol is advertised on the television, in magazines, and on billboards. Companies that produce alcoholic drinks spend a great deal of money on research to find out what appeals to young adults. One way these companies appeal to young people is to show adverts that feature animated animal characters such as frogs and ferrets.

Another effective advertising technique is to make it look as if you have to drink their product in order to have fun or to look cool. Alcohol companies show these adverts during television programmes that are popular with young adults. Alcohol companies also sponsor popular cultural and sports events.

Not every message in the media is pro-alcohol. Many organizations use the media to educate teenagers in the dangers of alcohol. THINK is the Department of Transport's drink drive campaign. It has produced some very shocking adverts to encourage young people not to drink and drive.

Some beer companies have used animal characters in their adverts to appeal to young people.

GUINNESS
IS GOOD FOR YOU

Effects of alcohol

When a person drinks alcohol, it is absorbed into the bloodstream through the stomach and small intestines. Once in the bloodstream, alcohol travels to the brain and other organs in the body. Alcohol affects the brain by causing it to release certain chemicals. These chemicals give the drinker a pleasant feeling. Alcohol also weakens the brain's ability to communicate with the body.

Alcohol's effect on a person depends on several factors. People who drink on an empty stomach or who are not used to drinking will feel the effects more strongly. Body size also makes a difference. Smaller people feel the effects more than larger people. In addition, each person's body chemistry is unique, so each person will feel the effects of alcohol in a different way.

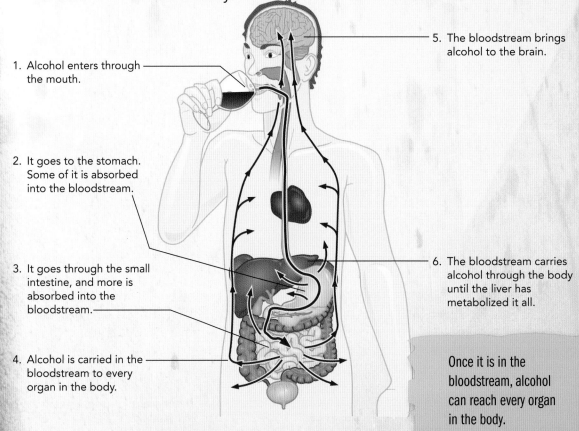

1. Alcohol enters through the mouth.

2. It goes to the stomach. Some of it is absorbed into the bloodstream.

3. It goes through the small intestine, and more is absorbed into the bloodstream.

4. Alcohol is carried in the bloodstream to every organ in the body.

5. The bloodstream brings alcohol to the brain.

6. The bloodstream carries alcohol through the body until the liver has metabolized it all.

Once it is in the bloodstream, alcohol can reach every organ in the body.

The average adult can **metabolize** one drink an hour. This means that it takes about an hour for the liver to break the alcohol down. Most adults who drink are social drinkers. This means they do not drink more than their bodies can metabolize.

Binge drinking

When people drink more than their bodies can metabolize, they begin to feel the effects of being **intoxicated.** How intoxicated a person becomes depends on how much that person drinks. People get very intoxicated, or drunk, when they **binge drink.** When people binge drink, they drink much more than their bodies can metabolize.

There is no agreed definition for binge drinking, but Alcohol Concern has defined it as having five or more drinks in a short space of time.

NEWSFLASH

Women metabolize alcohol differently than men. A recent study of men and women who weighed the same amount took place. It found that the women became more intoxicated more quickly than the men who drank the same amount.

Levels of intoxication

A person who has had an alcoholic drink will probably feel relaxed and sociable. Most people drink because they like this feeling. Their judgement and **motor skills** may be slightly impaired. These effects will increase as the person drinks more. Speech may become slurred and **reflex** time may slow down. The person's emotions are also affected, as is his or her sense of **inhibition.** They stop caring what other people think of them.

Heavy drinking

A person who has been binge drinking may have difficulty talking and walking. He or she may have poor coordination and reflexes, and feel sleepy. Alcohol irritates the stomach, so the person may vomit. The person may be confused and have concentration and memory problems. In addition, he or she may have inappropriate emotions such as extreme sadness or anger.

An alcoholic drink can make people feel relaxed.

Alcohol poisoning

A person who drinks a great deal may have **blackouts**. In extreme cases a person can die from alcohol poisoning. Alcohol poisoning occurs when a person drinks so much that the alcohol slows down his or her breathing and heart rate to dangerously low levels. A person who has alcohol poisoning may stop breathing or may choke or suffocate on his or her own vomit because the gag reflex is impaired.

People who drink excessively often suffer from a **hangover** the next day. People who have a hangover will likely have a bad headache and feel nauseous.

Top Tips

A person who has alcohol poisoning needs immediate medical attention. Here are tips for identifying alcohol poisoning:

- The person is unconscious and cannot be woken up.
- The person is breathing eight or fewer times per minute.
- The person's skin is cold and clammy and has a bluish tinge.

If you suspect alcohol poisoning, call 999 immediately!

Drinking too much alcohol in a short period can be very dangerous.

Drunk driving

Driving while intoxicated is very dangerous. Alcohol affects motor skills, reflexes, and judgement. Because alcohol affects people's judgement, they often do not realize how intoxicated they are. Even a small amount of alcohol can affect a person's driving ability.

More than 550 people in the United Kingdom die each year in alcohol-related car crashes. In 2004 there were more than 17,000 drink driving related casualties on the United Kingdom's roads.

Penalties are harsh for people who drink and drive. Drunk drivers can receive large fines, community service, and prison sentences. Their drivers' licenses are often suspended or taken away. Many drink drivers are young. A recent study showed that 6.3 percent of people aged 17–24 failed a breath test after an accident. The average for all ages was only 4.4 percent.

Case Study

Jason was drinking with his 15-year-old brother and some of their friends. On the way home, Jason lost control of his car. The crash killed his younger brother. Jason served four years in prison. Today he counsels teenagers on how to say no to alcohol.

Thousands of car crashes are caused by drunk drivers.

Roadside memorials are often left for people killed by drunk drivers.

Designated drivers

One way for people to avoid drinking and driving is to use a designated driver. A designated driver is a person who does not drink in order to drive other people home after a party or event. Some pubs and bars provide free soft drinks for designated drivers.

What do you think?

In some states in the United States, such as Texas, a person who kills someone because they were driving while intoxicated can be subject to second-degree murder charges. In 2006 a man who drove while intoxicated received a 30-year prison sentence for killing another man in a head-on collision. Some people think this is too harsh a punishment. What do you think?

Alcohol and health

People who drink a lot of alcohol over a period of many years may suffer from serious illnesses as a result. An estimated 33,000 people in the UK die from alcohol-related diseases every year.

Alcohol and the brain

Alcohol damages the brain and causes it to shrink. This brain damage causes memory loss, difficulty in concentrating, and **dementia.** For young people whose brains are still developing, this is especially worrying.

Alcohol damage to the adolescent brain can be permanent, causing life-long learning and emotional problems. Studies have found that teenagers who binge drink regularly have serious memory and learning problems. In addition, teenagers who drink often are more likely to have social problems and feel depressed. Alcohol is often a factor in teenage suicides.

A healthy liver (left) looks smooth, while the liver of a heavy drinker (below) is rough and lumpy.

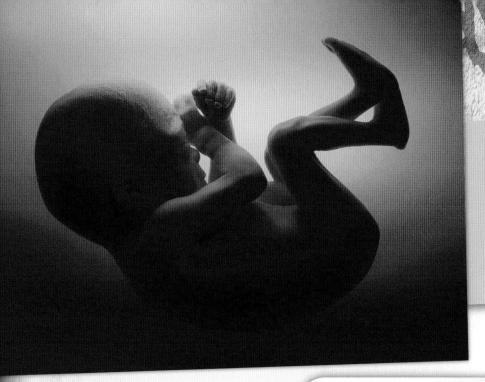

When a woman drinks during pregnancy, the alcohol can affect her unborn baby.

Alcohol and the body

After many years of heavy drinking, the liver can become damaged or inflamed. **Cirrhosis**, **hepatitis**, and other liver diseases kill tens of thousands of people each year. Alcohol also takes a toll on the digestive system. Heavy drinking can damage the **pancreas** and the stomach and cause them to become inflamed. Drinking alcohol can cause **ulcers**.

NEWSFLASH

An American Medical Association study took place in 2002. It found that an important part of the brain called the **hippocampus** is 10 percent smaller in teenagers who drink heavily than in teenagers who do not drink. The hippocampus plays a significant role in memory and emotions.

Some people who drink alcohol heavily suffer from poor nutrition and weight gain. This is because alcoholic beverages are high in calories but low in nutrients. Other heavy drinkers may become underweight because they skip meals in favour of drinking.

Alcohol can harm an unborn baby. When a pregnant woman drinks alcohol, she risks her baby being born with Foetal Alcohol Syndrome (FAS). Children born with FAS have lifelong physical, emotional, and mental problems.

Young drinkers

Teenagers and young adults are especially prone to binge drinking. Rather than drinking just a little alcohol with a meal, teenagers often drink in order to get drunk. Studies have shown that teenagers who binge drink are more likely to engage in other risky behaviours such as driving while intoxicated, using other drugs, and committing crimes.

Accidents, suicide, and violence are some of the most common causes of death for people between the ages of 16 and 25. Alcohol often plays a part in all three of these.

Case Study

Adrian, a university student, has seen the negative effect that drinking had on his uncle and cousin. He says he does not drink because of what he has seen and out of respect for his parents. Adrian is helping his nephew not to drink. He says that his true friends understand and accept that he chooses not to drink.

Playing football is a great way to have fun without alcohol.

Why teenagers drink

Like adults, many teenagers enjoy the feeling that alcohol gives them. Some teenagers drink alcohol to cope with stressful situations. Using alcohol to cope with stress is neither effective nor safe. There are better ways to reduce stress, such as getting enough sleep and exercise, maintaining a healthy diet, and having positive relationships with friends and family. If you are experiencing a high level of stress, you should talk to a trusted adult such as a teacher or parent.

Peer pressure plays a big role in teenage drinking. Teenagers may drink to fit in with their peers or impress others who they want to be their friends. Sometimes teenagers make poor choices because they feel they will be made fun of or rejected by their peers if they refuse to drink.

Teenagers also learn by example. Children who grow up in homes where alcohol is frequently consumed are likely to become drinkers themselves.

Peer pressure often leads teenagers to try alcohol at parties. Even if they do not want to drink, they may pretend to like it in order to fit in.

Alcohol addiction

A person can be a binge drinker or a heavy drinker without being addicted to alcohol. Only a small percentage of people who drink are **alcoholics**. Alcoholics have strong cravings to drink and cannot limit how much they drink once they start. In addition, alcoholics experience **withdrawal** symptoms if they try to stop drinking.

Several factors have been found to increase a person's likelihood of becoming dependent on alcohol. Researchers have found that alcoholism is **genetic.** This means that alcoholism runs in families. People who spend a lot of time around people who drink may be more likely to drink themselves and to become alcoholics. In addition, high levels of stress can increase the chances of a person becoming an alcoholic.

Alcoholism strains family relationships.

NEWSFLASH

A 2006 study in the United States found that children who start drinking alcohol before the age of 14 are more likely to become alcoholics than those who drink after 21. Nearly half of the young teenagers in the study became alcoholics, while only four percent of the older drinkers did.

The effects of alcoholism

Most alcoholics drink a lot of alcohol every day. Getting and drinking alcohol affects every aspect of their lives. Alcoholics often try to hide their addiction from their families. They may drink in secret, hide bottles, and lie about their drinking. Alcoholics are frequently moody and may be prone to outbursts of anger or violence. They are often not dependable, and spend a great deal of time either intoxicated or hungover.

A person who is addicted to alcohol usually cannot maintain healthy relationships. Alcoholic teenagers often have problematic relationships with their parents or guardians. Many alcoholics lose friends because of their drinking. They may not be able to keep their jobs because they drink while at work or miss too many days from being intoxicated or hungover.

Alcoholism can ruin a person's life.

Children of alcoholics

People who are intoxicated may neglect or mistreat their children. Children who grow up in homes with an alcoholic may feel anxious. They may be afraid of the alcoholic with whom they live when he or she is intoxicated. Children of alcoholics often feel angry, depressed, and confused. In addition, they may also have trouble trusting other people, since they cannot trust their alcoholic parent.

Some children of alcoholics feel responsible for their parent's drinking. Children with an alcoholic parent are often forced to take on adult caretaking roles. They may have to do household chores such as laundry and cooking, or even take care of a parent who has a hangover. Children of alcoholics often feel embarrassed about the parent's behaviour and might not invite friends to visit.

Case Study

Robbie grew up with an alcoholic father. He says it was like his father was two different people. Robbie wanted to spend time with his dad, but soon after he came home from work, his father would drink and turn into a person that Robbie did not like or feel safe around.

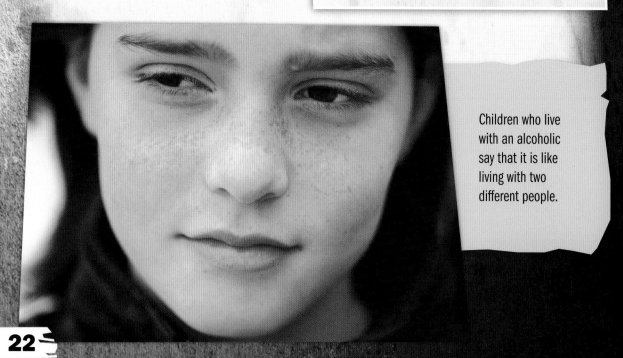

Children who live with an alcoholic say that it is like living with two different people.

Children of alcoholics often cannot depend on their parents.

Finding support

Children who live with an alcoholic need to remember that the person's alcoholism is not their fault. Nor can they fix the problem. Instead, these children should seek outside support from someone such as a teacher, doctor, or the parent of a friend. It is important for children with an alcoholic parent to have a safe place to go if their parent becomes violent while intoxicated.

Top Tip

If one of your parents is an alcoholic, sometimes it might feel like you need to take care of him or her. It is just as important to take care of yourself. Spend time with friends, doing things you enjoy. It can help take your mind off problems at home. Don't be afraid to share your feelings with a friend or trusted adult. Remember that you cannot cure your parent's alcoholism.

Treating alcohol addiction

Alcoholism is not curable, but it is treatable. Most alcoholics say that they still crave alcohol to some extent even after they have completely stopped drinking it. Many alcoholics cannot drink even a small amount without relapsing, or returning to their addiction.

Alcoholics are often in **denial** about their drinking problem. Recognizing and admitting that there is a problem is the first step in alcohol treatment. Family members and other people who care about the alcoholic can talk to them to help them realize the effects of their drinking. It is a good idea to get help and support from a professional counsellor when confronting an alcoholic.

Sometimes people realize that they have a problem on their own. Often this happens after a traumatic event such as a car accident. If you or one of your peers has a problem with alcohol, talk to a parent, teacher, counsellor, or other trusted adult.

Talking to a trusted adult can be the first step in dealing with an alcohol problem.

The only way to treat alcoholism is to stop drinking.

Detoxification

Once an alcoholic has agreed to get help, he or she must stop drinking alcohol and go through **detoxification** to rid the body of alcohol. Detoxification takes three to six days and may have to take place at a medical centre or hospital. During detoxification, an alcoholic experiences intense cravings for alcohol and withdrawal symptoms.

When the body is deprived of alcohol, an alcoholic can experience a wide variety of symptoms, including:

- feelings of restlessness, anxiety, irritability, or depression
- difficulty thinking clearly
- sweating and shaking
- headache
- sleeping difficulties
- nausea
- fever
- **hallucinations**
- **convulsions**.

Rehabilitation

Following detoxification, alcoholics may benefit from a rehabilitation programme. **Rehabilitation** programmes help recovering alcoholics by addressing emotional issues associated with drinking. They teach alcoholics new coping skills for dealing with cravings and staying away from alcohol.

Some alcoholics may need to go to an inpatient rehabilitation facility where they live for several weeks or months. In this environment there is no access to alcohol. Others may be able to live at home and visit an outpatient facility for rehabilitation. Some rehabilitation programmes are designed especially for teenagers and young adults.

Many recovering alcoholics need long-term support. A support group such as Alcoholics Anonymous (AA) or counselling can help keep an alcoholic from drinking again. Members of AA use a 12-step programme and offer support to each other. There are AA groups especially for teenagers. There are also AA groups for children and family members of alcoholics.

Case Study

Anna was 18 years old when she realized that she had a problem with alcohol. At first she tried to cut down on her own. She soon realized she could not control her drinking. Then she found a 12-step group and got the support she needed to give up alcohol for good.

Alcoholics Anonymous has helped thousands of people to stay away from alcohol.

True friends will never pressure you to drink, and will help you have plenty of fun without alcohol!

Prevention

There are many programmes that focus on preventing young people from drinking. These programmes educate teenagers about alcoholism and alcohol abuse. Often teenagers learn about the dangers of alcohol in school. Organizations such as Talk to Frank and Wrecked also help young people make wise choices about drugs and alcohol.

Drinking alcohol is dangerous for all children and teenagers. No one should drink any alcohol until they reach the legal age. People who are at risk of becoming alcoholics should consider not drinking alcohol at all, even when they are old enough to drink it legally.

Saying no to alcohol

It can be hard to say no when you are offered alcohol. But saying no is the only way you can protect your brain, health, and maybe even your life. Here are some tips to help you to stay away from alcohol:

- Avoid getting into situations where you might feel pressured to drink. Do not socialize with people who you know drink. Do not go to unsupervised parties.

- It is much easier to say no if you are not alone. Find a like-minded friend and stick together.

- Say no and then change the subject. Ask a question or suggest something else to do.

- Have a non-alcoholic drink already in your hand. People are less likely to offer you a drink if you already have one.

- Remember: It is okay to just say no, you do not owe anyone an explanation.

- Be polite, if possible. Stand up straight, use clear language, and a strong voice.

It is a good idea to have an answer ready if someone offers you alcohol. Try to find a reason to say no that is true for you.

"No thanks, I'm fine."

"No thanks, my parents will ground me for life if I come home smelling of beer."

"No thanks, I don't like the taste."

"No thanks, alcohol makes me sick."

"No thanks, my uncle died from alcoholism, so I don't drink."

If someone will not stop pressuring you, it is okay to be rude. You can tell the person to back off, or simply walk away. Sometimes it helps to talk to someone you trust such as an older sibling, teacher, or friend. Remember, your real friends will respect your decision not to drink.

Alcohol facts

- Drinkers start to outnumber non-drinkers by the age of 12.
- Sixty-five percent of pupils are between 13 and 14 years old when they have their first whole alcoholic drink.
- By the age of 16 nearly all young people (94%) have tried drinking alcohol.
- An estimated 33,000 people in the United Kingdom die from alcohol-related diseases every year.
- Each year in Australia approximately 3,000 people die as a result of excessive alcohol drinking and around 65,000 people are hospitalized.
- Each year more than 550 people in the United Kingdom die in alcohol-related car crashes.
- In 2004 there were over 17,000 drink driving related casualties in the United Kingdom.
- Alcohol kills more teenagers than all other drugs combined.
- Around 1,000 young people under the age of 15 years need emergency treatment for alcohol poisoning each year.
- The United Kingdom has some of the highest levels of drunkenness in Europe.
- In 2003, 68 percent of 15- to 16-year-olds in the United Kingdom reported being drunk at least once in the last year.

Teenage drinking causes thousands of deaths and injuries each year. You can save lives just by staying away from alcohol and encouraging your friends to do the same.

Glossary

addicted dependent on a particular substance, such as alcohol

alcoholic someone who is addicted to alcohol

binge drinking drinking a large amount of alcohol in a short period of time

blackout not being able to remember what happened while intoxicated

cirrhosis damage to the liver that can be fatal, caused by excessive alcohol use

convulsion sudden, uncontrollable shaking or movement of the body

craving extremely strong desire

culture way of life for a particular group or nation

dementia loss of intellectual functions

denial refusal to accept a truth

depressant substance that slows down the vital systems in the body

detoxification removing a poison from the body

ferment process of chemically changing a substance using micro organisms such as yeast

genetic relating to traits that are passed down or inherited

hallucination something that is seen or heard that is not really there

hangover feeling sick after being intoxicated

hepatitis inflammation of the liver

hippocampus part of the brain associated with memory and emotions

inhibition feeling of worry or embarrassment that keeps people from doing or saying whatever they want

intoxicated drunk

metabolize break down food

motor skill ability to use muscles effectively for movement

pancreas large gland behind the stomach that helps with digestion

peer pressure social pressure to behave or look a certain way in order to be accepted by a group

reflex the body's rapid and automatic response

rehabilitation return to a healthy condition and way of living

ulcer sore on the lining of the stomach that does not heal naturally

withdrawal unpleasant physical and emotional symptoms that occur when a person gives up a substance on which he or she was dependent

Further Resources

Books

Alcohol? (What do we think about), Jen Green (Hodder Wayland, 2001)

Drinking Alcohol, Pete Saunders and Steve Myers (Watts, 2004)

Jon Drinks Alcohol, Janine Amos (Cherrytree Books, 2002)

Websites

Talk to Frank
http://www.talktofrank.com/drug.aspx?id=166

Wrecked
http://www.wrecked.co.uk/

Al-anon/Alateen Australia
http://www.al-anon.alateen.org/australia/index.html

Organizations:

Alcoholics Anonymous
General Service Office
PO Box 1
10 Toft Green
York YO1 7ND
National Helpline: 0845 769 7555
Web: http://www.alcoholics-anonymous.org.uk/

Australian Drug Foundation
409 King Street
West Melbourne 3003
Postal: PO Box 818
North Melbourne 3051
Phone: 03 9278 8100, Fax: 03 9328 3008
Email: adf@adf.org.au
Web: http://www.adf.org.au

Index